THIS BOOK BELONG TO :

Hey, I am KnowledgeBird!
Are you ready to have fun!

This is a CIRCLE
The Circle has no sides

Let draw some
CIRCLES

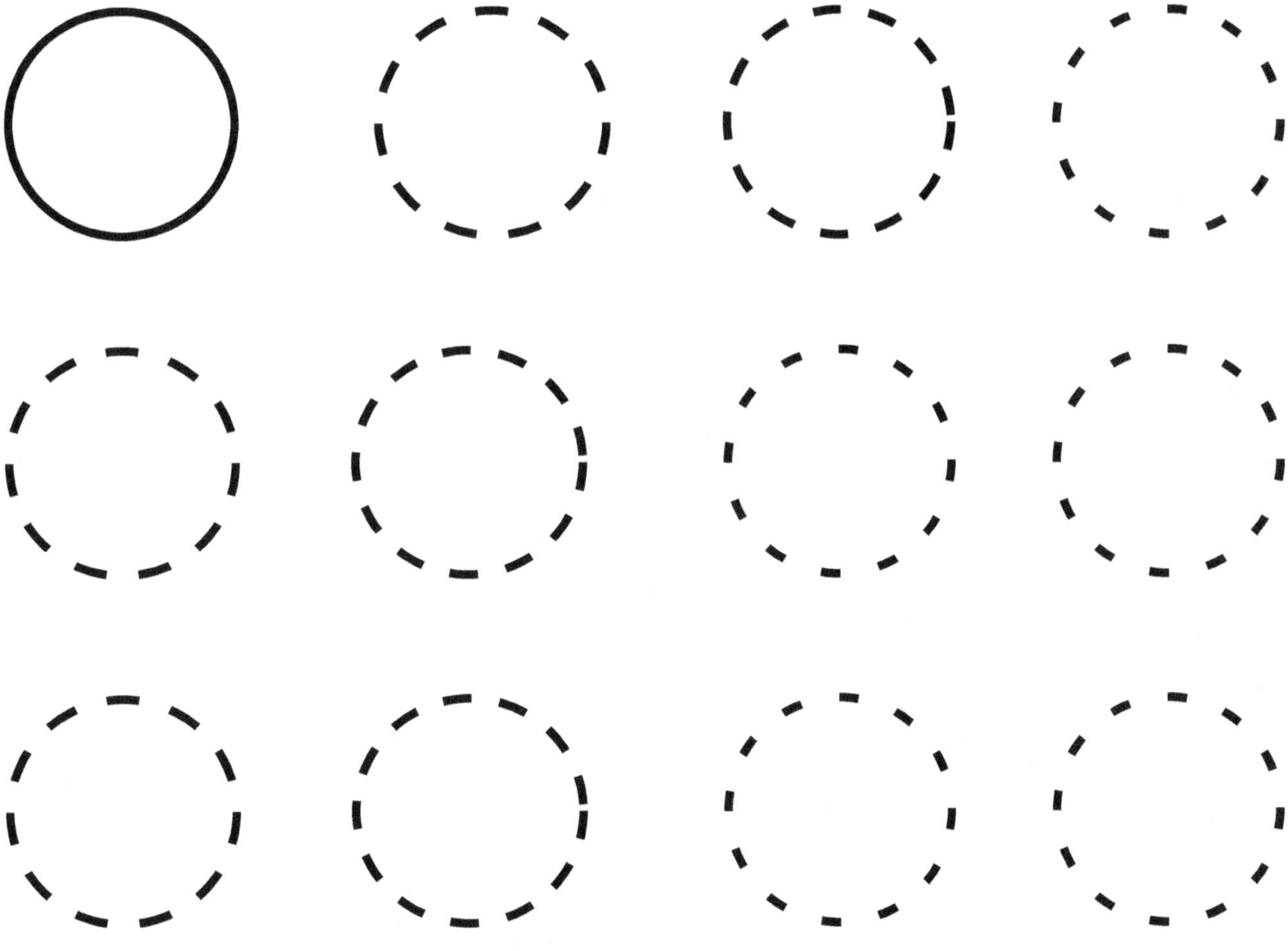

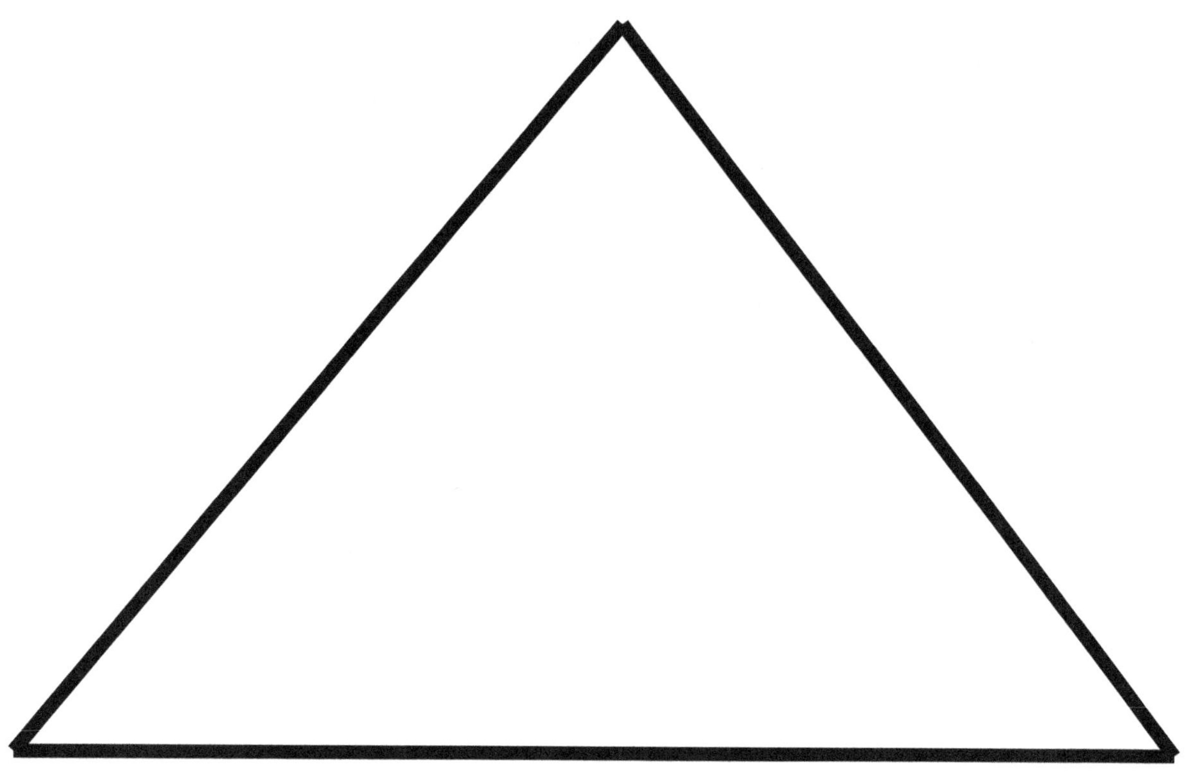

This is a TRIANGLE
The Triangle has 3 sides
and 3 corners

Let draw some
TRIANGLES

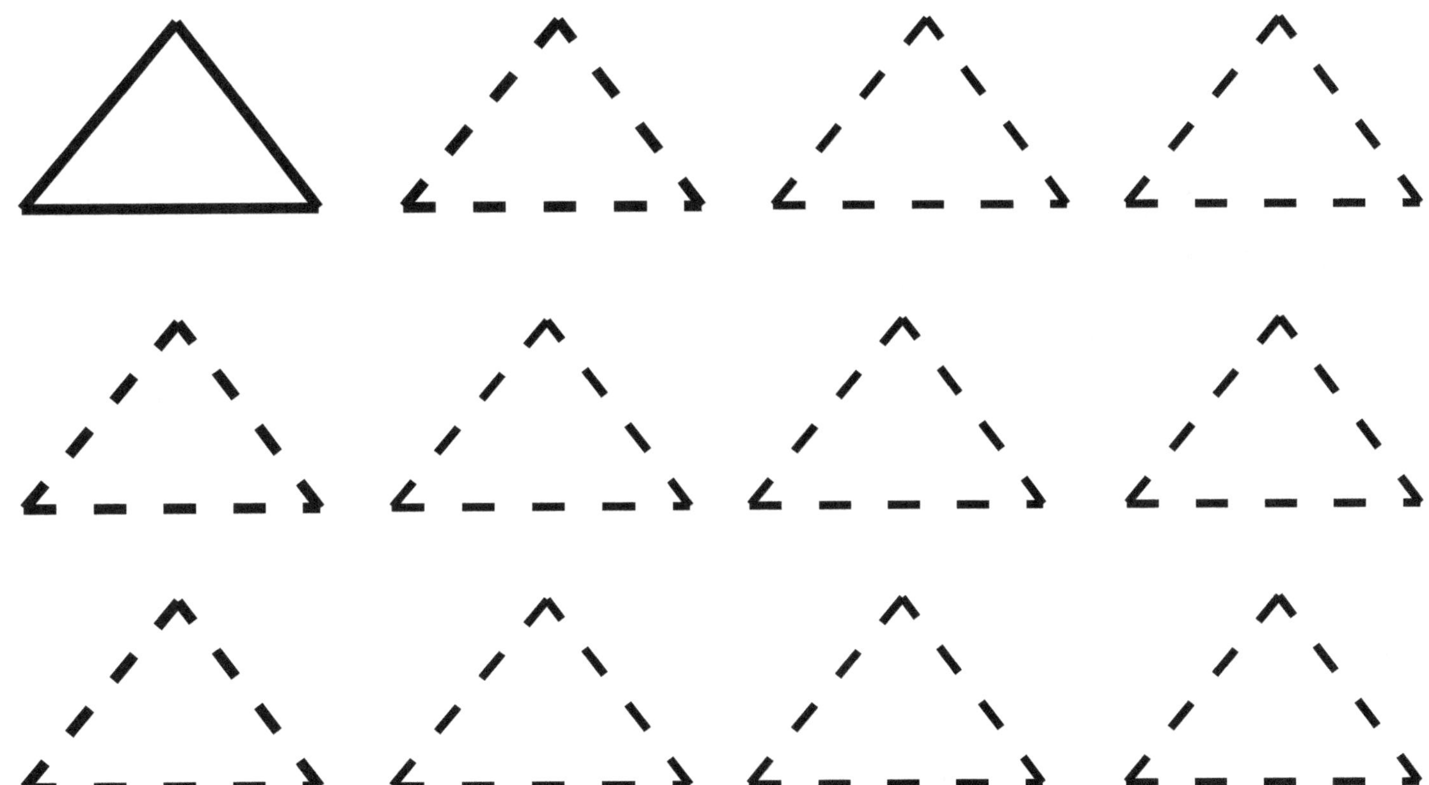

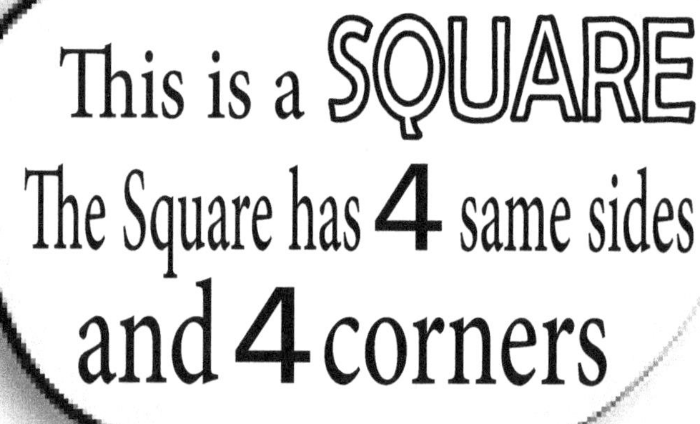

This is a SQUARE
The Square has 4 same sides
and 4 corners

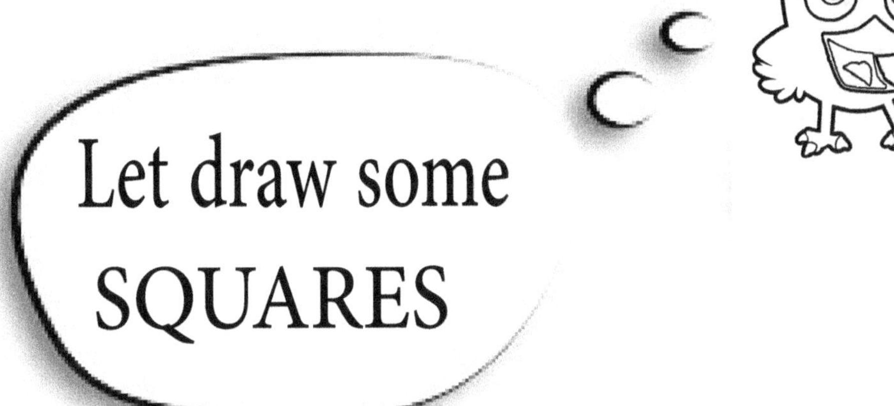
Let draw some
SQUARES

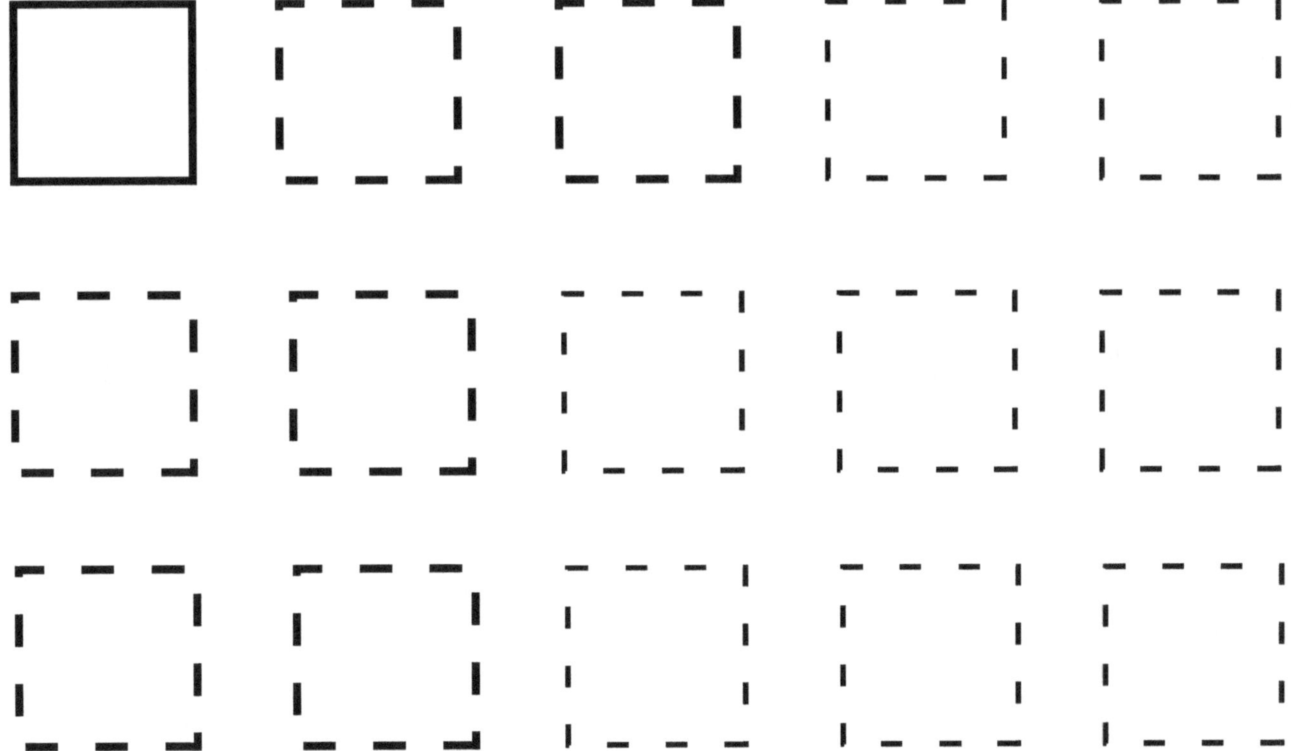

This is a STAR
The Star has 10 same sides
and 10 corners

Let draw some
STARS

This is a
MOON

Let draw some
STARS

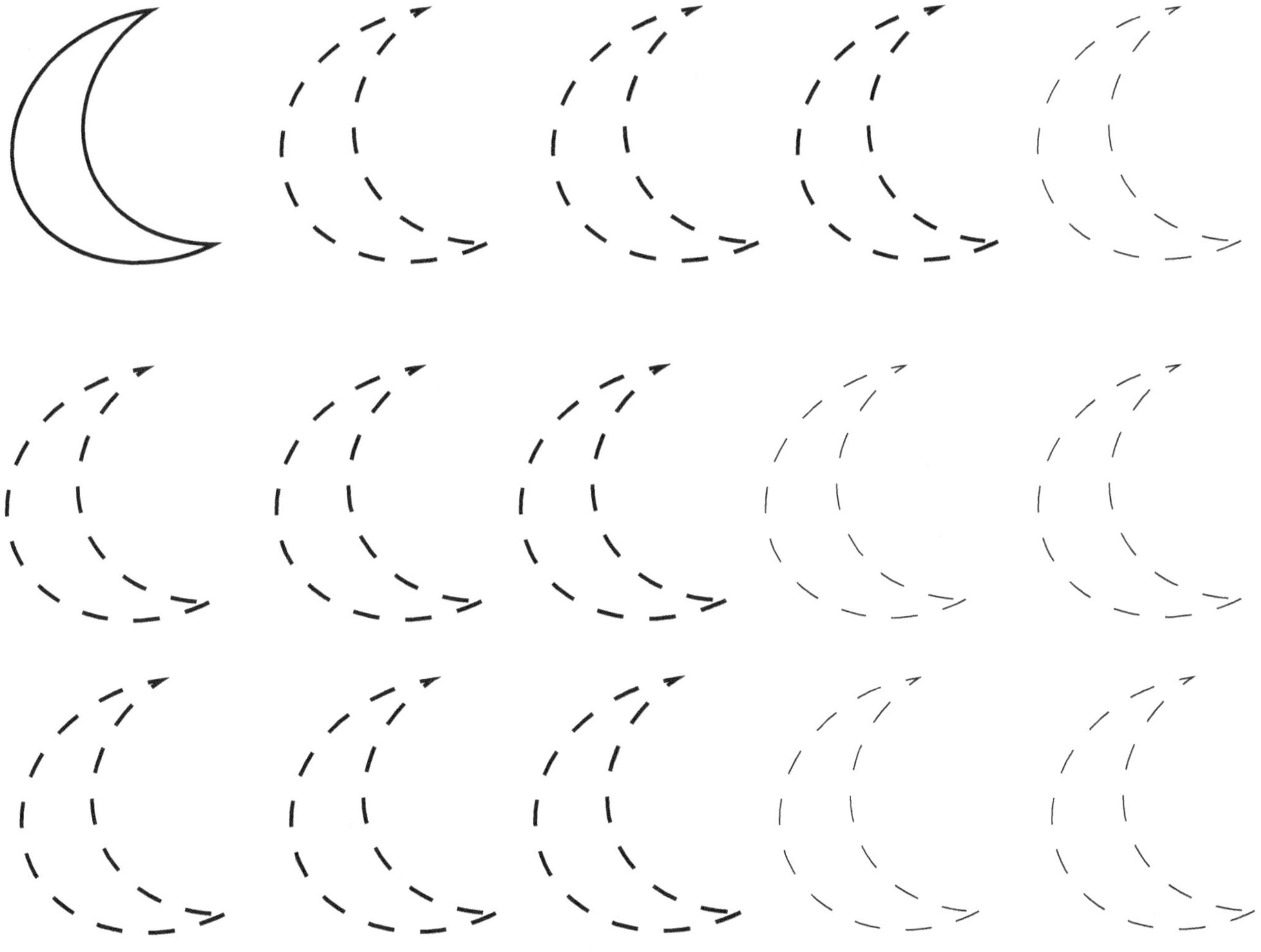

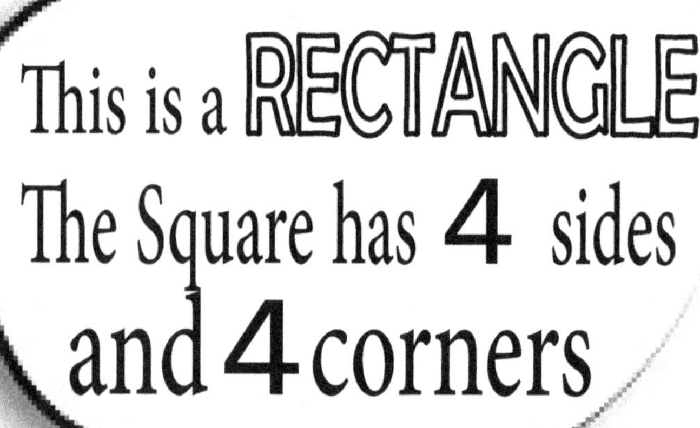
This is a RECTANGLE
The Square has 4 sides
and 4 corners

Let draw some
RECTANGLES

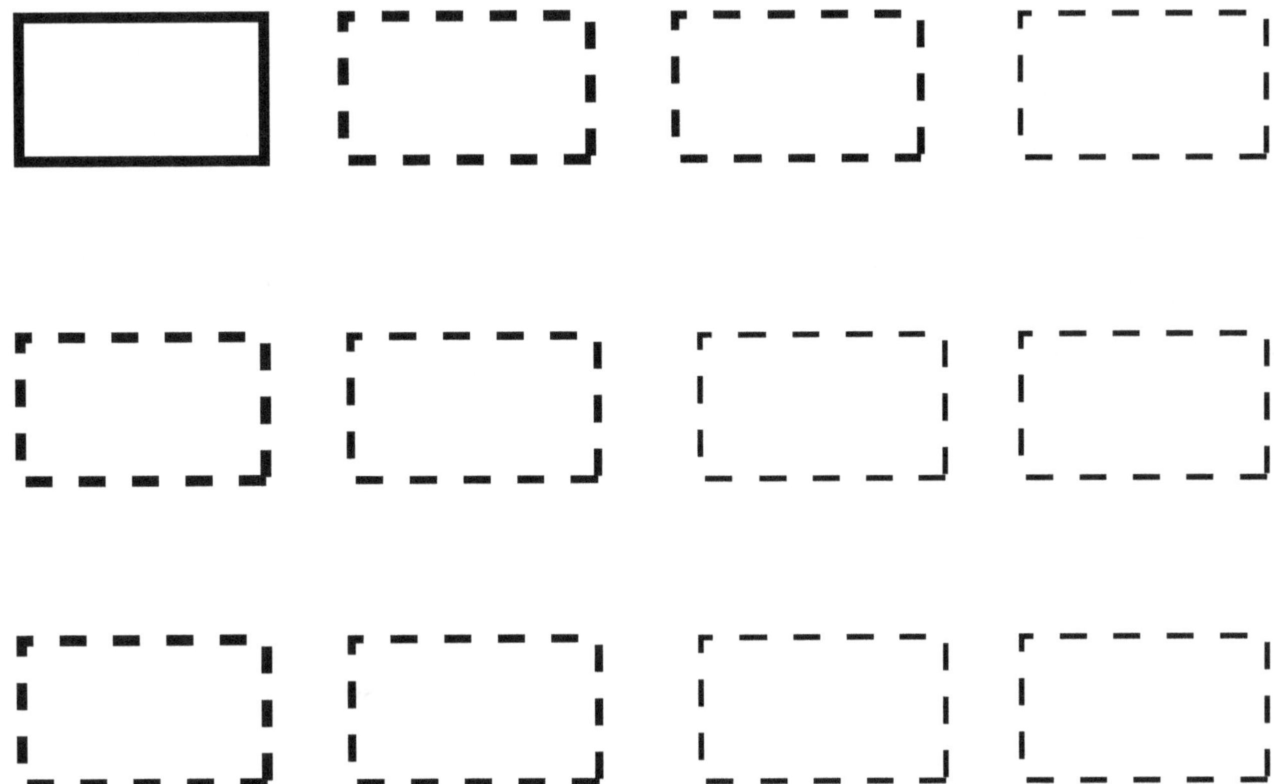

This is a PENTAGON
The Pentagon has 5 sides
and 5 corners

Let draw some
PENTAGONS

This is a HEXAGON
The Hexagon has 6 sides
and 6 corners

Let draw some
HEXAGONS

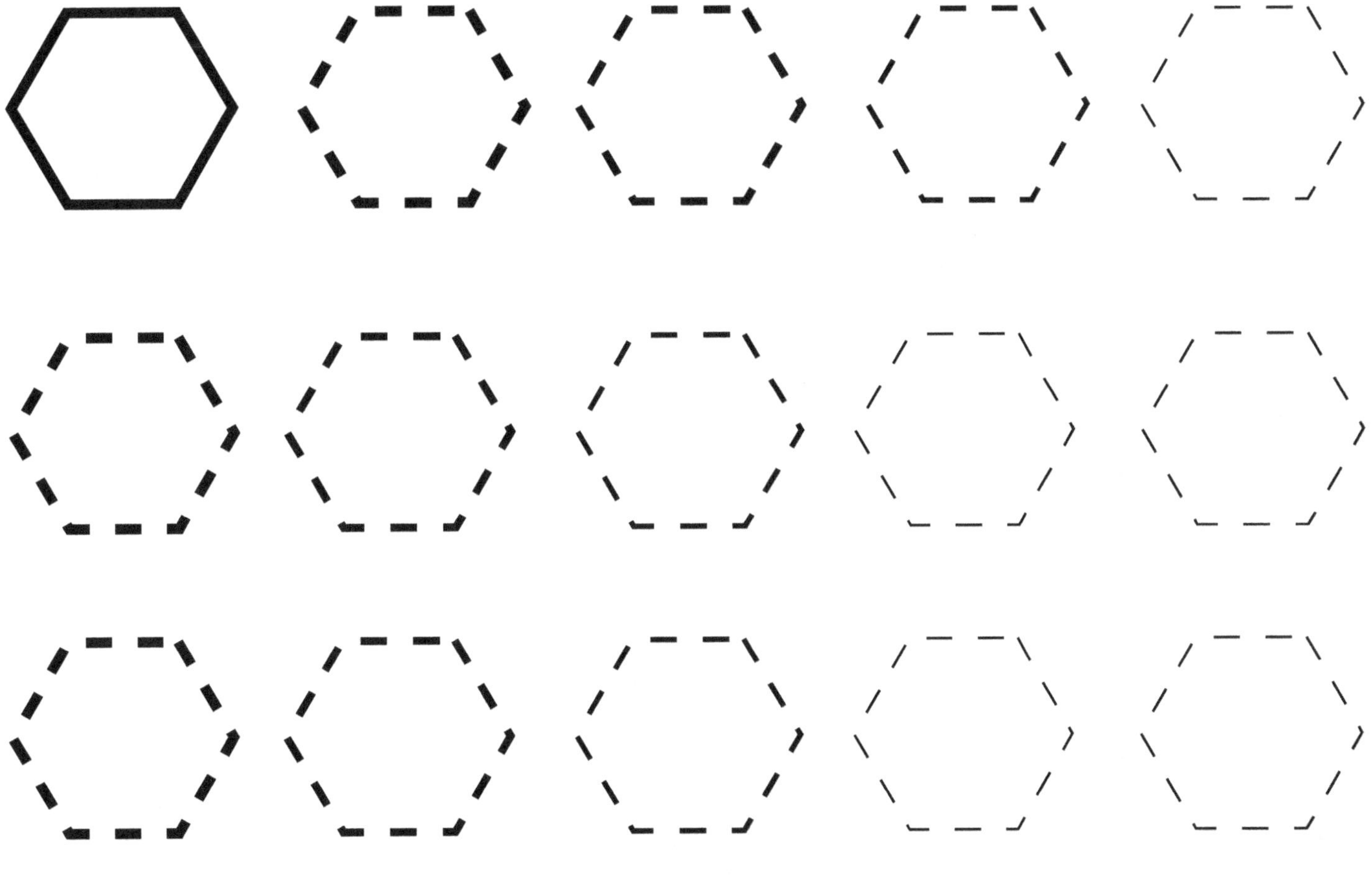

This is a OCTAGON
The Octagon has 8 sides
and 8 corners

Let draw some
OCTAGONS

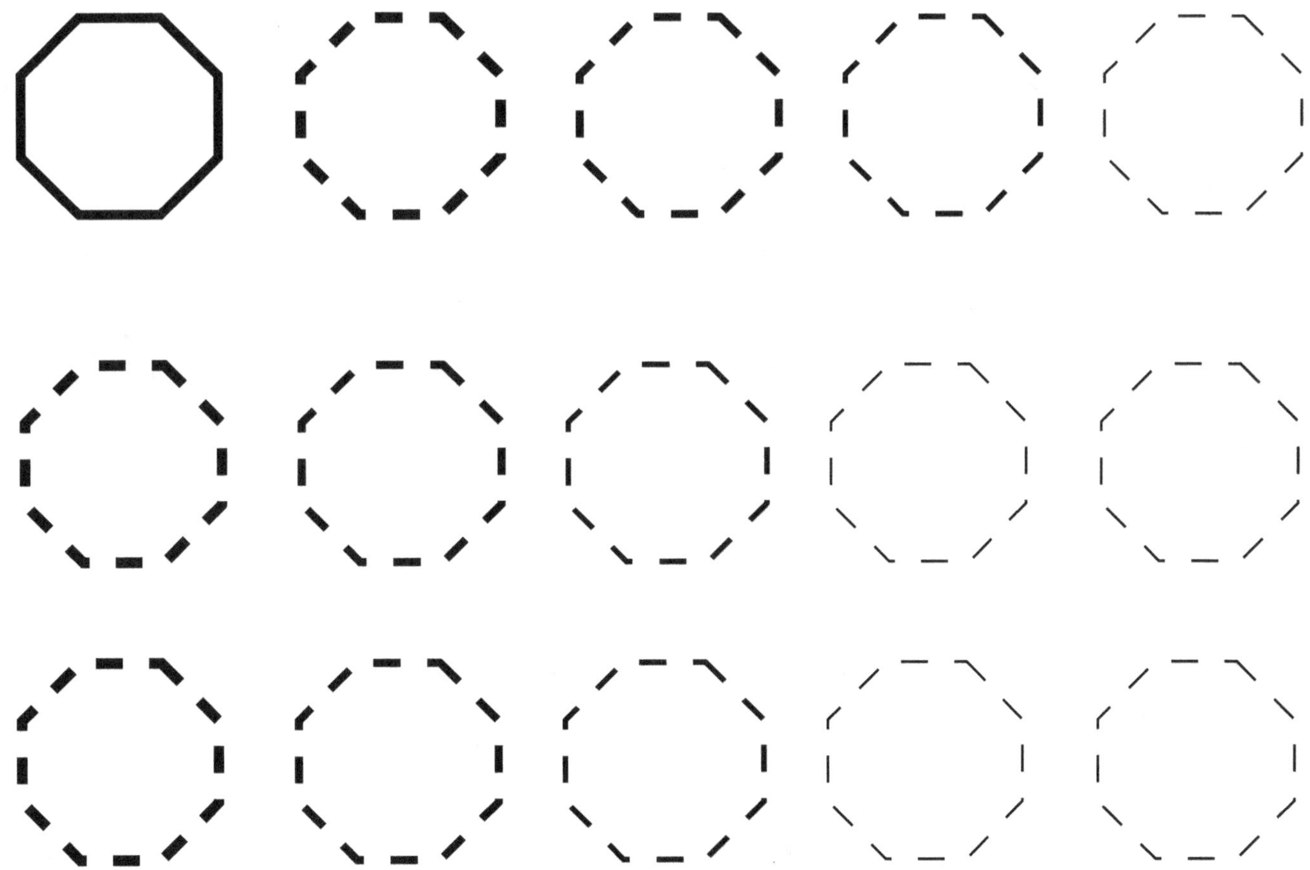

This is a DIAMOND
The Octagon has 4 sides
and 4 corners

Let draw some
DIAMONDS

This is a OVAL
The Octagon has no sides
and nocorners

Let draw some
OVALS

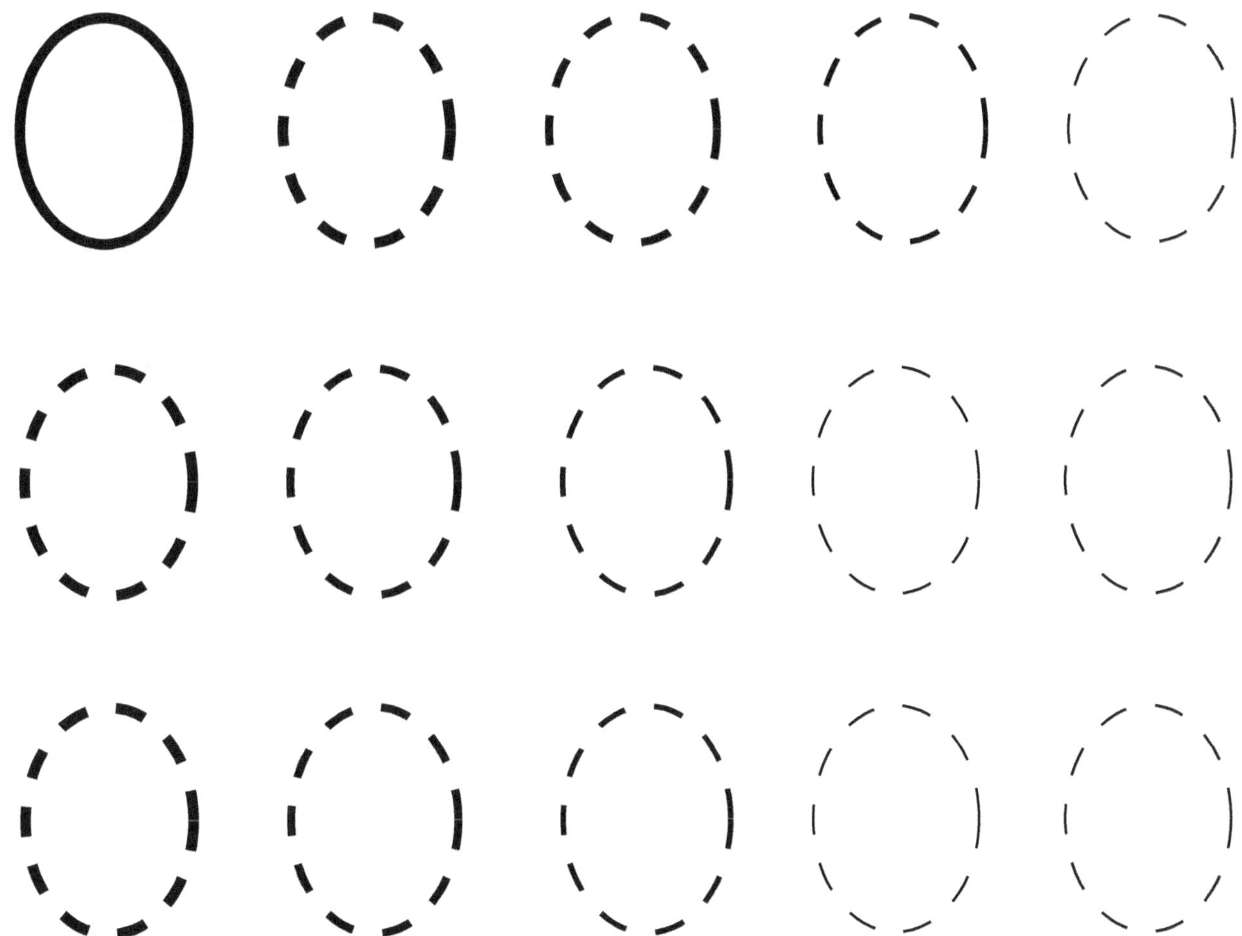

This is a
PARALLELOGRAM
The Parallelogram has 4 sides
and 4 corners

Let draw some
PARALLELOGRAM

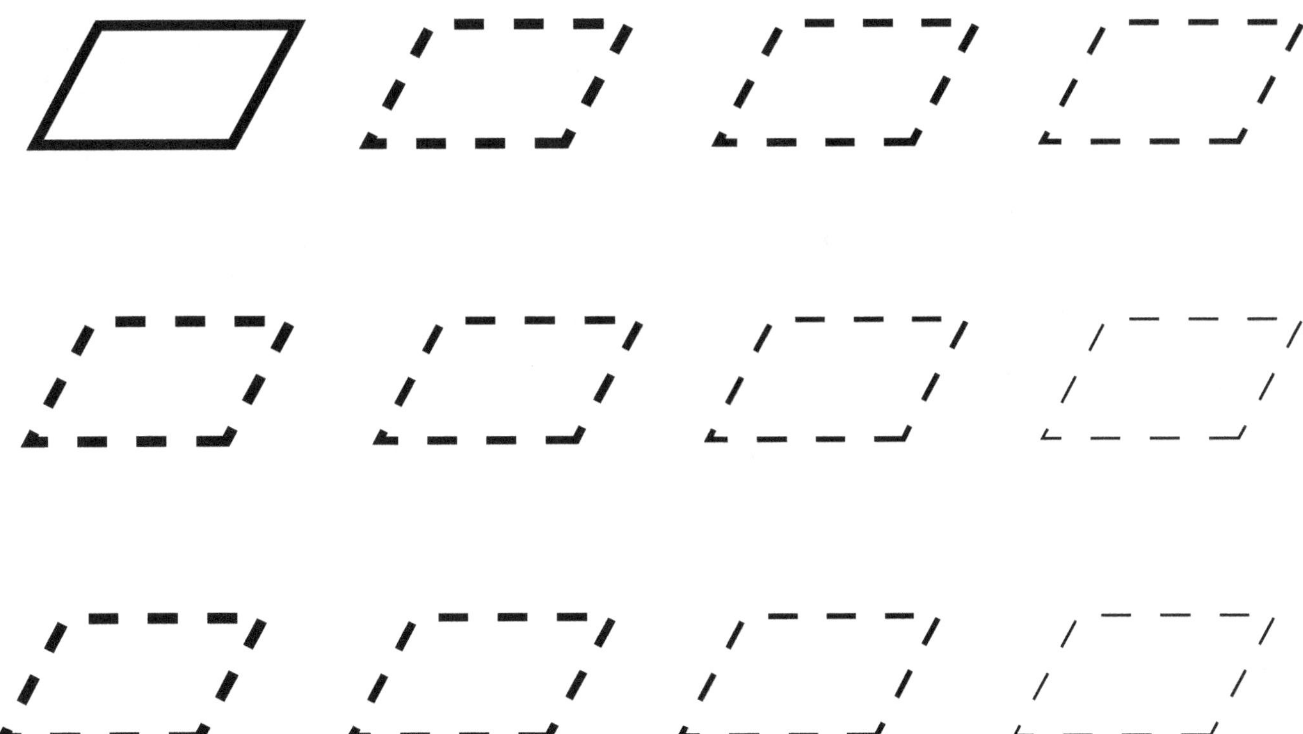

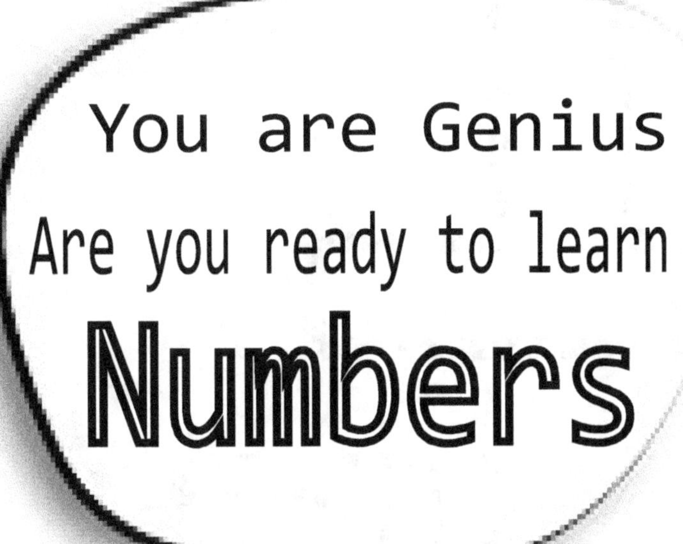
You are Genius
Are you ready to learn
Numbers

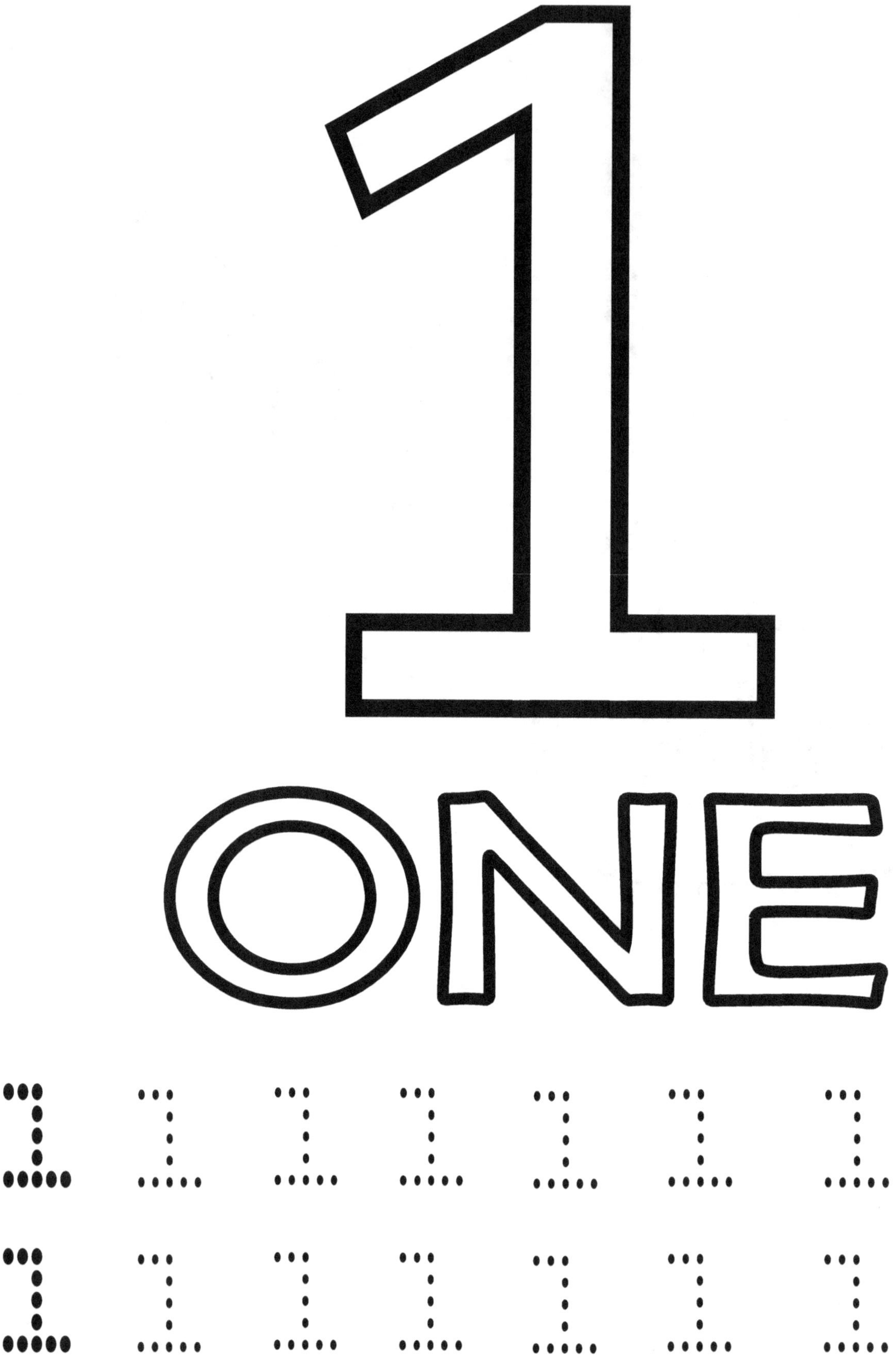

2
TWO
2 2 2 2 2 2
2 2 2 2 2 2

3

THREE

3 3 3 3 3 3
3 3 3 3 3 3

4

FOUR

6

SIX

7
SEVEN

8
EIGHT

9
NINE

10

TEN

10 10 10 10

10 10 10 10

11

ELEVEN

12

TWELVE

12 12 12 12

12 12 12 12

13

THIRTEEN

13 13 13 13 13

13 13 13 13 13

14

FOURTEEN

14 14 14 14

14 14 14 14

15

FIFTEEN

15 15 15 15 15

15 15 15 15 15

16

SIXTEEN

16 16 16 16

16 16 16 16

17
SEVENTEEN

18

EIGHTEEN

18 18 18 18

18 18 18 18

19

NINETEEN

19 19 19 19 19

19 19 19 19 19

20

TWENTY

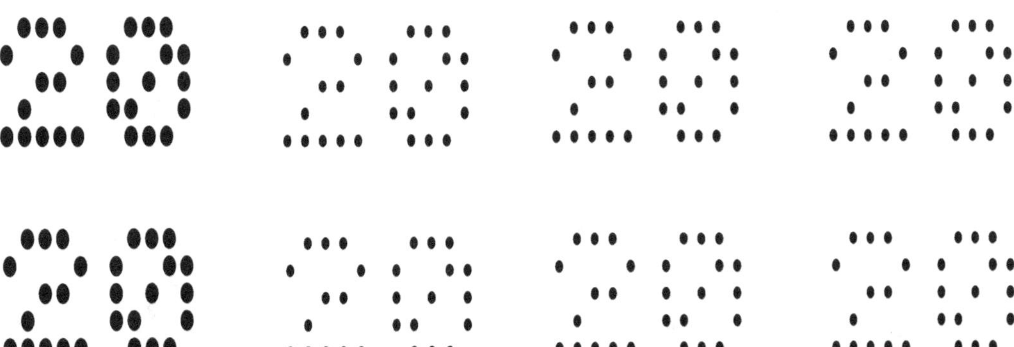

30

THIRTY

30 30 30 30

30 30 30 30

40

FORTY

40 40 40 40

40 40 40 40

50

FIFTY

50 50 50 50

50 50 50 50

60

SIXTY

60 60 60 60

60 60 60 60

70

SEVENTY

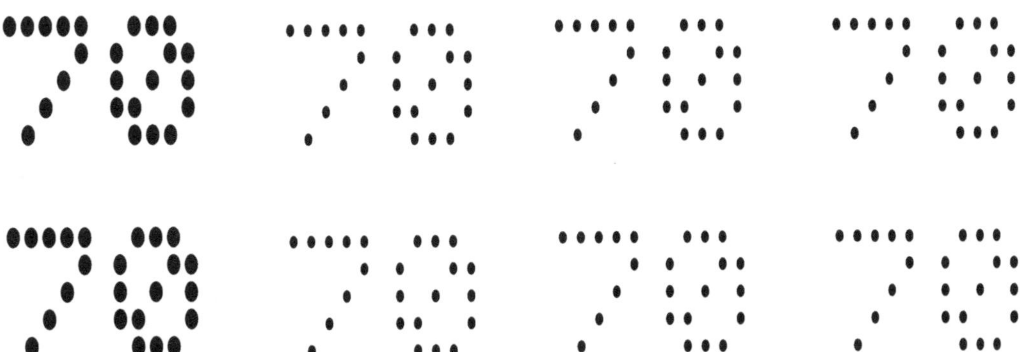

80

EIGHTY

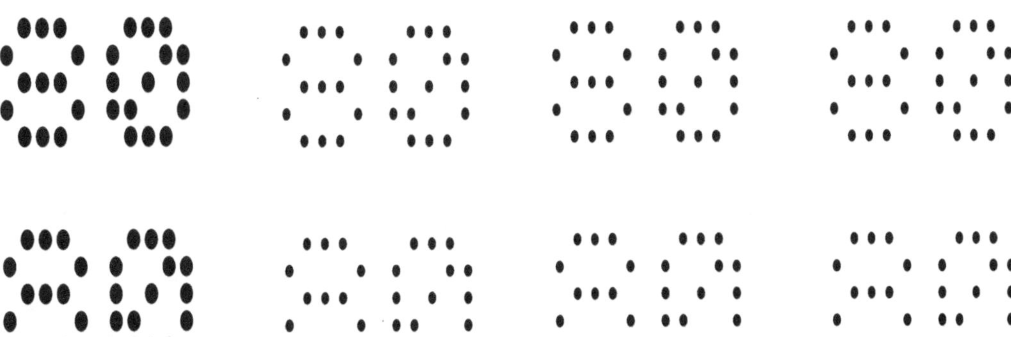

90

NINETY

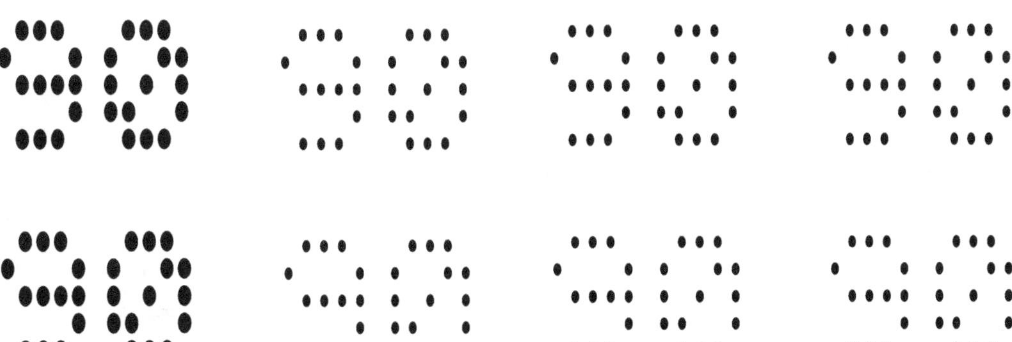

100
ONE HUNDRED
100   100   100
100   100   100

1000

ONE THOUSAND

Awesome you are good learner
Check ours other books
on amazon by visiting
our author page :
KnowledgeBird Publishing
or our website :
/https://knowledgebirdp.blogspot.com